Let's Look at Monster Machines

John Allan

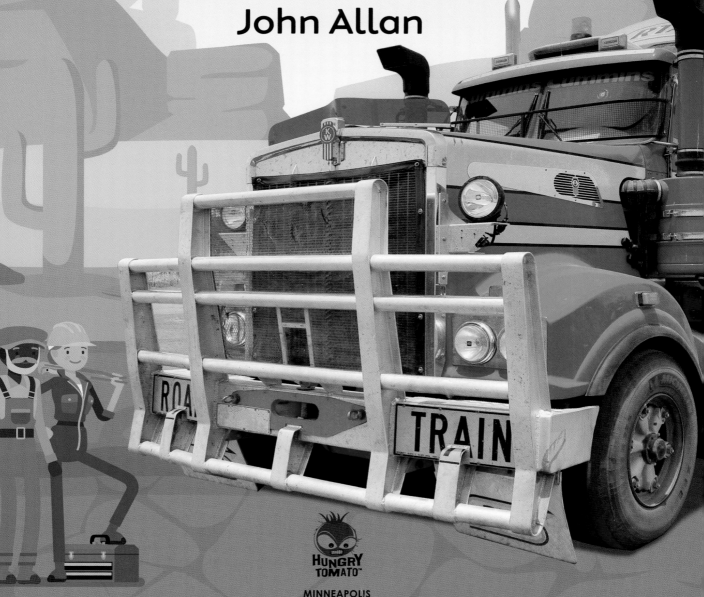

HUNGRY TOMATO™

MINNEAPOLIS

Hungry Tomato®
A division of Lerner Publishing Group, Inc.
241 First Avenue North
Minneapolis, MN 55401 USA

For reading levels and more information,
look up this title at www.lernerbooks.com.

Main body text set in Fibra One Alt.

Library of Congress Cataloging-in-Publication Data

Names: Allan, John, 1961– author.
Title: Let's look at monster machines / John Allan.
Description: Minneapolis : Hungry Tomato, 2019. |
Series: Mini mechanic | Audience: Ages 6–9. | Audience:
Grades K–3.
Identifiers: LCCN 2018052143 (print) | LCCN 2018058967
(ebook) | ISBN 9781541555327 (eb pdf) | ISBN
9781541555310 (lb : alk. paper) | ISBN 9781912108169
Subjects: LCSH: Machinery—Juvenile literature.
| Vehicles—Juvenile literature. | Construction
equipment—Juvenile literature.
Classification: LCC TJ147 (ebook) | LCC TJ147 .A45 2019
(print) | DDC 621.8—dc23

LC record available at https://lccn.loc.gov/2018052143

Manufactured in the United States of America
1-45933-42827-1/18/2019

Contents

The Mini Mechanics

We are the mini mechanics.
Welcome to our workshop.
We work on some amazing vehicles.
Here are a few of the tools we use to
fix them.

A good mechanic needs to keep their tools tidy.

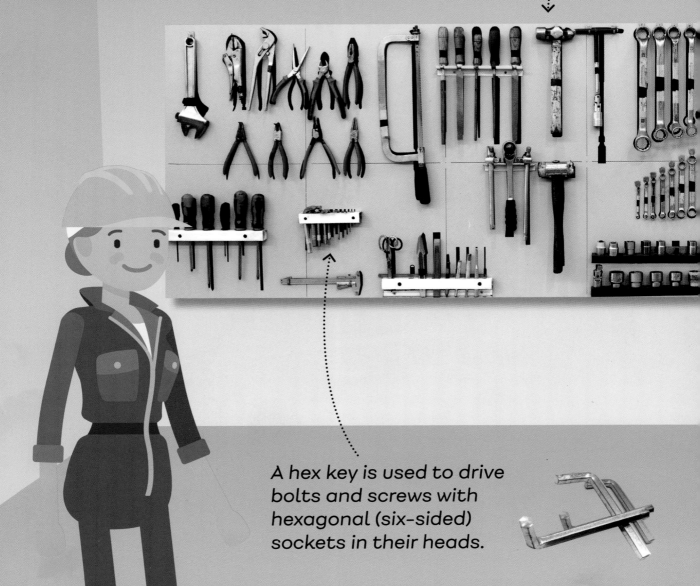

A hex key is used to drive bolts and screws with hexagonal (six-sided) sockets in their heads.

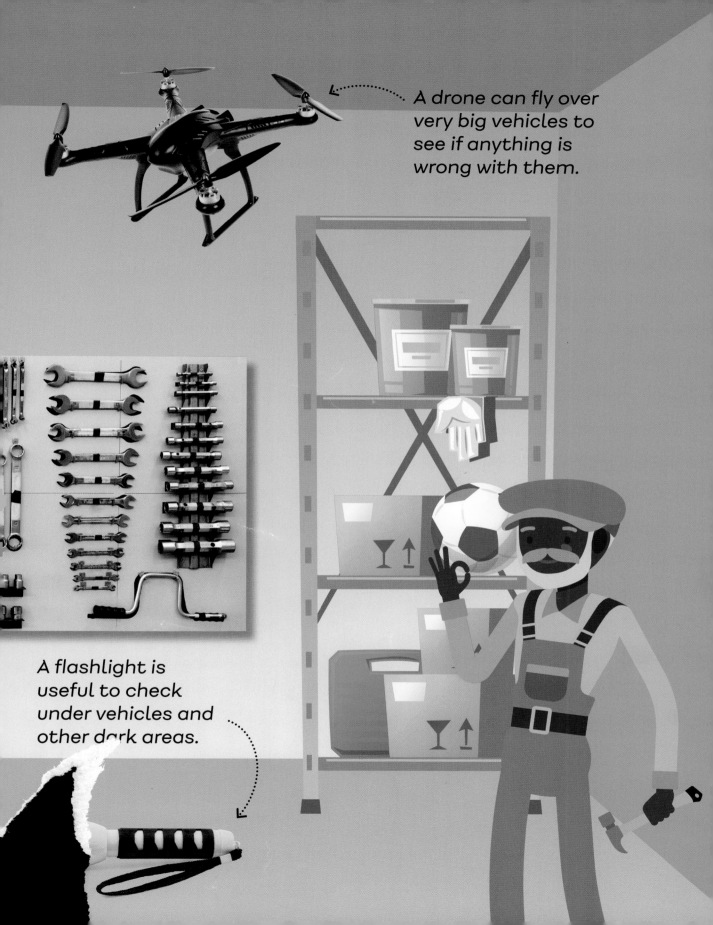

A drone can fly over very big vehicles to see if anything is wrong with them.

A flashlight is useful to check under vehicles and other dark areas.

Large Mobile Crane

Truck cranes move around on wheels. They have one cab for controlling the crane and another one for driving the truck.

This crane is lifting a heavy concrete support.

Metal legs called outriggers stabilize the crane.

This is the boom. It can reach to the top of a six-floor building.

Monster Tractor

Giant tractors work in the big fields of North America. They can work for up to twenty-four hours without stopping.

Some wheat fields in America are so big it takes an hour to drive from one end to the other.

The eight wheels on this tractor stop it from sinking into muddy ground.

Tractors often work at night. They need lights so their drivers can see where they are going.

Australian Road Train

These monster trucks are the kings of the road in Australia. They drive long distances to deliver their goods.

The powerful engine helps the truck haul heavy loads at fast speeds.

This road train is driving through part of Australia.

They can carry enough fuel to drive 1,000 miles (1,600 km).

Bucket Wheel Excavator

This enormous machine is a bucket wheel excavator. It is used to dig for coal.

These cables lower the bucket wheel until it touches the ground.

When the wheel turns, buckets scrape up the coal.

The wheels can scrape up 40,000 buckets of coal in one day.

13

Giant Floating Crane

Some cranes float on water.
They are used to work on oil rigs
and build bridges over water.

This crane is lifting part of a new ship.

Floating cranes use strong cables to lift huge ships out of the water.

NASA Crawler-Transporter

This is the largest transporter in the world. It carries rockets and spacecraft to their launch pads.

Crawler-transporters move slower than a person walks when carrying a load.

This crawler has carried a spacecraft to its launch pad.

The crawler has tracks at each corner to drive it.

BelAZ 75710 Monster Truck

This giant dump truck carries loads in mines. Its body can tilt so that the loads slide out.

This truck can carry up to 440 tons (450 t) of rocks. ·········

The driver has to climb this ladder to reach the cab. ···

The huge wheels are as tall as a grown-up.

75710

Dodge Power Wagon

This is the giant Dodge Power Wagon—
the largest car in the world.

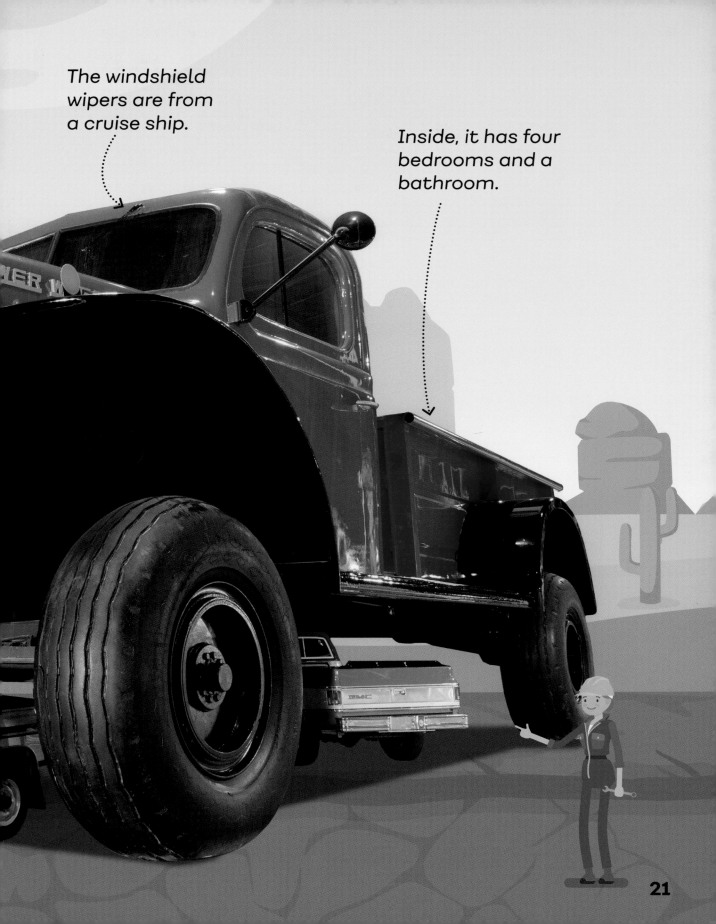

The windshield wipers are from a cruise ship.

Inside, it has four bedrooms and a bathroom.

21

Antonov An-225 Plane

This is the longest plane in the world.
It is 275 feet (84 m) long.

Only one of these incredible planes flew in 2018, but more are planned to fly in the future.

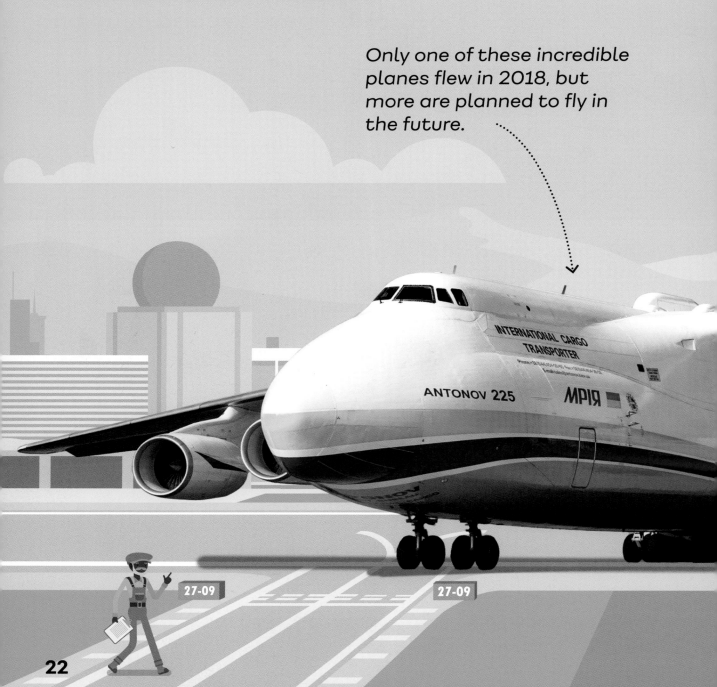

The nose of the plane has been raised to load a helicopter.

Six jet engines power the plane through the air.

The plane lands and takes off on thirty-two wheels.

Glossary

boom: a movable arm, as on a crane

cab: the part of a vehicle where the driver sits

excavator: a heavy construction vehicle

mining: removal of coal or minerals from the ground

oil rigs: structures with equipment to remove oil from underground

stabilize: to make steady

wingspan: the distance from the tip of one wing to the other

workshop: a place where things are made or repaired